TOMORROW IN THE BATTLE

A Play

by Kieron Barry

samuelfrench.co.uk

THINKING ABOUT PERFORMING A SHOW?

There are thousands of plays and musicals available to perform from Samuel French right now, and applying for a licence is easier and more affordable than you might think

---

From classic plays to brand new musicals, from monologues to epic dramas, there are shows for everyone.

Plays and musicals are protected by copyright law so if you want to perform them, the first thing you'll need is a licence. This simple process helps support the playwright by ensuring they get paid for their work, and means that you'll have the documents you need to stage the show in public.

Not all our shows are available to perform all the time, so it's important to check and apply for a licence before you start rehearsals or commit to doing the show.

LEARN MORE & FIND THOUSANDS OF SHOWS

Browse our full range of plays and musicals and find out more about how to license a show

www.samuelfrench.co.uk/perform

Talk to the friendly experts in our Licensing team for advice on choosing a show, and help with licensing

plays@samuelfrench.co.uk   020 7387 9373

Acting Editions

BORN TO PERFORM

Playscripts designed from the ground up to work the way you do in rehearsal, performance and study

---

Larger, clearer text for easier reading

Wider margins for notes

Performance features such as character and props lists, sound and lighting cues, and more

---

+ CHOOSE A SIZE AND STYLE TO SUIT YOU

  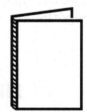

STANDARD EDITION	SPIRAL-BOUND EDITION	LARGE EDITION
Our regular paperback book at our regular size	The same size as the Standard Edition, but with a sturdy, easy-to-fold, easy-to-hold spiral-bound spine	A4 size and spiral bound, with larger text and a blank page for notes opposite every page of text. Perfect for technical and directing use

LEARN MORE | **samuelfrench.co.uk/actingeditions**

Other plays by KIERON BARRY
published and licensed by Samuel French

Numbers

FIND PERFECT PLAYS TO PERFORM AT
www.samuelfrench.co.uk/perform

ABOUT THE AUTHOR

Kieron Barry was born in Stratford-upon-Avon. He survived a disastrous education at Glebelands School in Cranleigh and went on to take degrees at the University of Durham and Goldsmiths' College, London.

His plays include the verbatim drama *Stockwell,* which enjoyed two sell-out runs in London. It was described by *The Times* in its five-star review as "more gripping than anything else to be seen in the London theatre" and by the *Daily Express* as "stark, stunning...deeply poignant...one of the most important plays of the year." The play prompted Barry's nomination for the Charles Wintour Award for Most Promising Playwright at the London Evening Standard Theatre Awards.

He is also the author of the one-act comedy *Numbers,* described as "sharp and funny, terrifying and inspiring" in Lucy Kerbel's book *100 Great Plays For Women* where it appeared alongside plays by Oscar Wilde, Tennessee Williams and Euripides.

His other plays include *Black Soap, Cumquats, Stories For Boys,* and *Lord Beckington (90) Reads From His Award-Winning Romantic Memoirs.*

www.KieronBarry.net
www.Facebook.com/KieronBarry.net/

AUTHOR'S NOTE

I once attended a performance of medieval music. After a lengthy sequence of unaccompanied vocal motets, a musician without warning strummed a single chord on a lute. Hardly the most lascivious of instruments, yet the effect was dazzling. The room all but gasped, as though a large tin of paint had been upset.

I became intrigued by the power of small effects in a desaturated aesthetic. Having just finished a piece of political verbatim theatre, I wanted to write whatever the opposite of that was; something pure and almost poetic, in which a single moment of overlapping speech – or the touch of two characters – might burst like a firework.

Another curiosity chimed pleasingly with all this; how to convey on stage not just action but interior sensation. Thus was I led to the monologue.

Many in the theatre are faintly biased against the monologue form. Ever obstinate, this emboldened me, as did seeing a masterpiece of the genre, Conor McPherson's *Port Authority*. Oblique, spellbinding and nothing but monologues. So I knew it could be done. And I could not find another way to bring fully into the light two murky and recurring preoccupations: our own perplexing conception of moral duty and the capricious zigzag of sexual desire.

I have never understood sex. Its discovery, like the dawning of one's religious faith, initially promises a life of joyful communion. Instead, both often bequeath journeys of unbearable loneliness. As a motive, sex appears flimsy and abstract in contrast to the quickly-grasped logic of, say, trade or revenge. As a problem, it is not only unsolvable but unclassifiable, like pain. In even the most well-ordered of homes we occasionally see desire thrashing its tail and insisting on its weird, destructive supremacy.

All too commonly and all too late we realise that the acts which have defined us did not seem to be choices at the time, still less choices with a moral component. Rather they were a series of instinctive thrusts propelling us towards what we want, or what we think we want, or whatever lies mysteriously behind that. The play attempts to put words to these wordless impulses and to dramatise that which is usually silent and invisible.

It is perhaps, when all's said and done, a meditation on the impermanence of sexual joy and the impossibility of moral triumph. How strange that even the most straightforward of quests in life – wanting things to be good – proves to be a storm-lashed crossing at night towards what dispiritingly looks less and less like a safe harbour.

Kieron Barry
2017

STAGING AND PRODUCTION NOTES

In rehearsal, the principal questions asked by directors and actors are the most sensible and obvious: where are these characters as they recount and relive their experiences, to whom are they doing so and why? The text offers no answers. Like running down stairs, the play works until one starts to wonder how.

(The only other regular question concerns the shard of glass in Scene 5. Again, the significance of this is not clear beyond giving a brief sense of uneasy premonition.)

Almost no stage directions have been included in the text. Directors must feel confident in fashioning the play to their own vision. The staging may be kept abstract and undefined, reflecting the opacity of the characters' location. Alternatively, with sets or tableaux, a more solid world may be illuminated either throughout or in glimpses – the fall from the bridge, for example, or the boy under the surgeon's knife.

Handel's *Eternal Source of Light Divine* is referred to at the end of Scene 16. Directors are strongly advised to include a substantial section of this short work. It stands almost in lieu of an interval, creating a moment in which the play is briefly suspended in mid-air. The recording made by trumpeter Tine Thing Helseth and soprano Isa Katharina Gericke is particularly recommended, the trumpet and voice heartbreaking in their counterpoint.

A NOTE ON THE TEXT

Simultaneous dialogue is indicated by the "/" symbol.

Tomorrow In The Battle received its world premiere on
17th August, 2012, at the Stageworks / Hudson theatre
in Hudson, New York, in a production directed by Laura
Margolis with the following cast of characters:

Simon   **Timothy Deenihan**
Anna   **Celia Schaefer**
Jennifer   **Danielle Skraastad**

WITH THANKS TO...

The author wishes to thank all the actors who made such valuable contributions to the development of the play, especially Tamsin Greig, David Morrissey, Danielle Skraastad, Alexander McConnell and Allison Threadgold. Likewise thanks are due to director Sophie Lifschutz, dramaturgs Ella Wrenn and Adrian Fear, and producer Anna Murphy. Thanks also to Portland Stage in Maine and Kitchen Dog Theater in Dallas for their workshops of the play.

For Chris and Elizabeth

CHARACTERS

SIMON – male, perhaps 50s
ANNA – female, perhaps late 40s
JENNIFER – female, perhaps 30s

The action of the play takes place in
the present day, mostly in London.

Scene One

SIMON Matt has already made it across and is waving like the
pissed-up tosser he is from the other end of the bridge.
Shouting the usual nonsense. He's done that thing of pulling
apart his bow tie, partly to prove he's a rebel, but partly – by
showing it's real, not one of those pre-tied ones – to prove
he's part of the establishment.

By the time we'd left the Formal we'd got through seven
bottles of wine between the three of us. And now here we
are. Midnight at the bridge.

It's Oscar's turn, and I'm after Oscar. He gets up on the
railing thing, a thin sort of parapet, and already he's a bit
unsteady. I say, "Look. If you run, you're less likely to fall
off than if you walk, 'cos you'll be more scared and alert."

Which I still think is logical.

The bridge is about a hundred foot long and it's about a
hundred foot above the water. But tonight it looks as though
the drop goes on forever. The parapet itself is about eight
inches wide.

Oscar's getting ready, but then he flashes me a look of total
fear, he looks about twelve. He doesn't belong with us, really,
Oscar. I remember him crying at a Floreat dinner once. Not
hunched over and sobbing or anything, just sitting upright
with a face-full of tears, God knows why. People around him
throwing bread at each other, ignoring him. But we're the
big boys, Matt and I, it's still a case of that, even at medical
school if you can believe it. And I really do think he likes
us. For whatever reason.

I look at him up on the bridge and I want to say, This is
stupid, we're just being stupid, let's just leave, let's go home,
and I want to pull him down and give him a hug – I'm serious
– and say everything'll be OK, just stick with it, you'll have
a good life, you don't need the approval of idiots like us.

That's what I want to say. What I *actually* say is, "Just hurry up and do it, will you."

I turn away, to suggest contempt, and I hear his steps start up – off he goes, the clip-clip of his dutiful stride – until, about halfway across, the rhythm dissolves into a tight clutch of semiquavers, the scuff and scrabble of his grooveless soles on the grainy shine of the asphalt, and I turn and I see his arm jerking out, jutting and elbowy – out goes the arm and I realise he's afraid of landing on the concrete of the bridge, that's what he's worried about. The horror of falling to his left, falling *off* the bridge itself hasn't even crossed his mind, and so he leans back the wrong way, out over the water, way out, and for one second nothing moves except his feet against the parapet, trying to hold on as if they were hands.

And then down he falls, headfirst and backwards.

Scene Two

ANNA Some evenings, before we go out, Simon will say: "Please don't tell them your job is making nuclear weapons."

His idea of a joke. We don't *actually* make them. (I *think* he knows that.) We just buy them from the Americans. But it is frustrating, telling people, and the first thirty seconds of every conversation are always the same. Hiroshima, mushroom clouds, Dr Strangelove.

I say: "We're not the Ministry of Attack. We're the Ministry of Defence." They're not interested, of course.

The entire British nuclear arsenal is carried by four submarines. We've no missiles on dry land. They're all out at sea, under the water, patrolling the world. Each submarine carries four missiles, and each missile contains twelve warheads, and each warhead can kill about thirty million people.

The intention is not to *use* these missiles. That would be unimaginable. Yes, they're *designed* to be used, and they're *capable* of being used, but they're a *deterrent*, in other words they only exist to stop other countries attacking us.

Now obviously if they're to be an effective deterrent, other countries really must believe that we intend to use them, and that's why frankly we *have* to intend to use them.

I know that's confusing: being able to wipe out any country on Earth makes the world a safer place. But it's true. It does.

Scene Three

SIMON I'm superstitious. Most surgeons are. On a good day I save someone's life. On a bad day I kill them. So it makes sense deciding each morning which foot's going to touch the ground first.

If I have to operate that day, Anna will massage my back for twenty minutes first thing. The truth is I don't need it, but I think she does. She says it's to relax me, she says she can see me starting to tense, but in fact she's seeing me start to concentrate, starting to become unsurprisable.

She's careful to warm the oil first with the heat of her palms, not wanting to make me jump. I patiently wait for her to finish, and when she does she turns me on my side and lies behind me, knotting her fingers together at my stomach.

People don't need to *be* beautiful. They just *are* beautiful. I tick off Anna's quirks one by one, all her odd, loveable confusions and embarrassments.

I look at her hands, soft and useless. And I think of the scalpel, cold and knowing and doing such good.

You don't *really* save anyone's life. You just keep them going for a few more years. They're carrying around the wrong heart, the heart of a stranger. They know it doesn't belong.

The patients all die prematurely, but so do the surgeons, in our case because we start so late. All surgeons are inexperienced, even the old ones. We have such a short distance between starting out and slowing down. It's like medieval love, which they say flowered with such intensity because puberty and death were separated by such a small gap.

I'm now in the golden hour, though, with everything at its peak. This started last summer, when I famously transplanted the heart of a baby, a baby just ten hours old, with a heart the size of a peach stone.

Scene Four

ANNA I was up in the attic. (We call it an attic.)

I'd fallen asleep downstairs earlier, quite by mistake, and I had that confusion you get when you wake up and it's starting to get dark. I wandered up here and sat down and opened a few boxes, pushing my hands into the papers and lifting a few at random as a child does with autumn leaves. They're all letters, letters to me. From grandparents, friends, names I've forgotten, although their letters are fizzy with excitement about seeing me next term.

Simon has kept no letters, but makes up for this with other heirlooms. He has a Nazi pistol that he used to keep up here with a whole trunk of other Second World War stuff. It's a Luger which his stepfather had almost unbelievably commandeered off a German officer in North Africa – I say unbelievably because this was a man so mild he wouldn't start his airline meal until all passengers had been served.

When his stepfather died, Simon took the gun from the attic and put it in his bedside drawer. I knew this was his way of trying to be close to him, but he never admitted this, it was just a private little thing he did. But I wanted to be included, so I asked him: "Why are we keeping an antique pistol in the bedroom, darling?"

"In case of civil war," he said, and kissed me.

Outside the light was decaying, the exact time of day Simon and I would walk at his parents' house in Dorset, that trapezoid in our history when he was still at medical school and I was finishing my PhD. The fields, our muddy wellingtons and cold ears, piling back to the farmhouse and the smell of toast, and him running his hands over me in the woody, Aga'd kitchen, telling me how beautiful I am. "Stop it," I'd say, "they could come in at any minute."

Now, in the blackening glass, I see I'm looking old. I've left the radio on downstairs, and as I listen to the music I hug my knees and imagine how the camera would start spinning round me in the film version of my life.

Oh yes, I was beautiful once.

Scene Five

SIMON It was Anna's idea. She got the tickets from work. But then she rings and says she's running late, and *then* she rings and says she's not going to be able to make it at all. "I'm already here," I said, "what am I supposed to do?" "Just try and enjoy it," she said. Enjoy it? It's an opera. I've been up for fifteen hours and it hasn't even started yet.

So there I am in Floral Hall.

And a woman walks in.

JENNIFER Here's why I'm here.

Last night started out fairly normally. Was bought drinks by some dude in a bar in Farringdon. Bit of a strapper, good chin, could have been from Australia. Or the West Country. Somewhere like that. I gleefully braced myself for a night of lovely working-class sex.

And so it was. He knew he was out of his depth socially, bless him, although I'll give him this, he could sustain an erection in front of an intelligent woman, and how many can boast that? I couldn't help noticing, though, he started swearing halfway through. "Oh fuck! Oh shit!" Why are you swearing? What we're doing is already X-rated. If you want sex *and* profanity why don't I just shoot myself in the head as well? Get a bit of violence in there too.

However. The strangest thing happened when I booted him out afterwards. Normally when they stagger off I exhale and rejoice, free at last to chew gum or snore or eat anchovies straight from the can. But not last night. Last night I panicked. I'm sorry. I did. No one was around. I realised no one was ever around.

I looked out at East London's ambiguous, replaceable sky, and I recalled that line from Pavese: "No one ever lacks a good reason for suicide." I filed the thought away, in the kind of place you keep job offers you've turned down over the years.

I also remembered Goethe's last words: Mehr licht. More light.

I was about to file those as well, when I suddenly thought, hang on; I'm crying. I'm actually crying. I hadn't cried since 1994, which for me was that year at school when your nose starts to grow and no other part of you does. Bugger me that was an awful time; I just turned up one day with a honk like Bill Clinton's. I thought: if my tits were growing like this thing I'd be the ruler of this place, but there you go.

I'm Head of Global Sales and Client Service. I got a scholarship to St Paul's, five As at A-Level and a Star First with Biochemistry Prize from Imperial College London. I need someone with a bit of heft, someone craggy and established, someone who wouldn't look out of place with a baton on the cover of a *Deutsche Grammophon* record. I'm tired of changing people. I want to be changed. I want someone I can be afraid of.

That's why I'm here.

SIMON There's that moment when Christ spins round and says, Who touched my cloak? And they say, Well, we're in a crowd, everyone's touching everyone. But he's right. There's two hundred people here coming and going, but when she walked in it was as if someone had opened an orange.

And with the confidence of the truly knackered I think: I'm going to talk to her.

JENNIFER When people look at me they tend to look at me in *this* eye. But you've gone for *this* eye. It does make a difference, because no face is symmetrical – the brain assembles a symmetrical face using just the half it's looking at, so someone will look completely different depending on which eye you look into.

SIMON After a few moments I lean my hand on the wall behind her, so she's almost nestled against my arm. I ask her about her work.

JENNIFER It's a two-person firm. I'm the mover, Alex is the
shaker. Or should that be the other way around? The point
is this. He hired me to go out and shake the hands – oh,
yes, so I'm the *shaker*. Impress the new clients. They like
me. I think because I'm a girl. In the financial sector we're
almost as popular as money.

Alex is a trader. He started in the eighties as a go-between
at the New York Stock Exchange. Now he's here, and he's
brilliant. Investors want an eight percent return. Alex
generally gives them eleven. And they say thank you.

I move around Europe – oh, so maybe I *am* the mover –
hunting down funds, ushering in the flow of money. I'm
client-facing and gregarious, the kind of girl hedge-fund
managers and high net worth individuals love to sit next
to. Men who've sold the nineteenth century family business
and now need some advice on what to do with the hundred
million. Men for whom it's not "*fi*-nance', it's 'f'*nance*".

But that's not me. That's just what I do.

SIMON Later, I take my seat as the house lights pale and the
music starts. I begin to wonder what it means – what music
means. Nothing, presumably, but I try to focus on it, see if
I can follow it, if there's some sort of argument I can make
sense of. But I can't, it's just a series of sounds, and they
only mean what they are.

Scattily she'd torn a bit of paper off and written her number
on it. In the darkness I feel the ragged edges of it with my
thumb. Easy enough to rip it up, chuck it away and off she
goes, thrown untraceably back into the infinity of London.

JENNIFER That night I wake up and feel something odd in my
mouth. When I take it out I see it's a piece of glass, just a
very small little triangle of broken glass. Yet as my tongue
scans my teeth and gums I detect no trace of blood.

Scene Six

ANNA I am the bearer of bad news. So bad, in fact, that I close the door behind me.

It's just me, and Sir Adam. And an oil painting of Sir Adam.

So here goes.

"There's a problem with the hardware. Could be a big problem."

This is the plan to renew our nuclear deterrent. It's what my career is all about. The one big event I was born at the right time to play a major part in. Updating Trident. In simple terms, the missiles are obsolete and they must be replaced. Parliament's approved our proposed budget, and we've agreed the sale with the Americans.

Except it's not so simple. I've just noticed an incompatibility in the match of one of Lockheed's systems to ours. Doesn't sound like a big deal, doesn't look like a big deal. But we have bought the wrong system, and we should have checked. In three months we give evidence to the Select Committee on the final costs. Should be a formality. But that was when it only cost one hundred and thirty billion. Now we could end up spending *real* money. And that's the kind of mistake that ends careers.

Someone should have noticed it, someone should have thought to ask. One of those things that's no one's fault, it's just everyone's fault. But there's only one man at the top.

When Sir Adam hears this he crumples, he can already hear the portcullis slamming down, locking him out of the one big remaining job – Cabinet Secretary. And he'll be doomed to roam Whitehall, an outsider with the mark of Cain. The man who bought the wrong missiles. The man who should have checked.

But he pulls himself together. That's the kind of man he is. "Who else knows about this?" he asks me.

"No one. Yet."

"What would happen," he asks, "if we gave the old figures to Parliament?"

"We... I don't understand."

"Later on, when it's all gone through, we could always just say the Yanks never told us. Their fault."

"But it's going to come out eventually."

"Sure, but that would be down the line."

By which he means when he's already in the top job.

But that would mean lying to Parliament.

Sir Adam looks out over St James's Park and thinks for a bit.

"Why don't you go up to the Clyde," he says. "Have a look at things first-hand. You've never actually seen the fleet, have you?"

Scene Seven

JENNIFER We have to meet for lunch near his work. That's how important and busy he is. It's a small restaurant on Rugby Street, off Russell Square. I get there first, and sit in the banquette facing out. Half the people in here must be doctors. It's probably the safest restaurant in London to start choking in.

A man approaches me, and I think it's him, but it's not. He's impressive, though, and so confident that it takes me a while to realise he's chatting me up. I say "I'm waiting for someone," but he gives me his business card with his four initials embossed in very dark blue – M. R. L. K., and I find I'm beginning to like the small scar that runs across his left cheek.

He leaves, and I'm left alone. I'm reflected everywhere, in the mirrors that line the walls, in the chrome of the lights, the shine of the cutlery, the bowls of the wine glasses and the curve of the bottle.

And I say his name three times: Simon. Simon. Simon. And he appears, and I feel something leap in my womb.

SIMON John Lennon's killer said that before the shooting he was waiting outside the Dakota building, and half of him was praying that Lennon would come back so he could shoot him, and the other half of him was praying that Lennon wouldn't come back, because if he did he knew he'd shoot him.

That's what it was like trying not to phone her, that's how it felt trying to walk away from the phone, until it was in my hand, not to call her but to return it to its cradle after I called her. That's how it happened.

JENNIFER I had bought him a pair of cufflinks from a small shop in the Burlington Arcade. What was I thinking? I just had this urge to spend money on him. I then took them back about an hour later, but then I changed my mind again and bought them back. So I have them with me, gift-wrapped in my bag, but as soon as he arrives I realise the whole idea's stupid and I don't get them out.

SIMON I tell her I don't drink at lunchtime. True, but not the whole story. I don't actually drink at all now.

JENNIFER I insist on paying, and as I look for my card he sees the gift-wrapped cufflinks and says, "What's this? Presents on a first date?" And I realise he's joking, he assumes it's not a present, it can't be, why would it be? It's not even a date, of course, and so I immediately say it's my little niece's birthday, and he says "Oh, what have you got her?"

And I say: "Cufflinks."

Later that afternoon I throw them into the Thames, but as I do so I manage to convince myself that for some reason he can still see me, this is like an hour after we said goodbye at the restaurant, but I can't shake the idea off, so I make it look as though I'm tripping up, and then I have to follow it through and act like I'm disappointed that they've gone overboard.

Scene Eight

SIMON We don't know when we'll get a heart that he can take, so I sit him down and try to explain. It's actually easier doing that with children than with adults. They're credulous.

He's ten years old, bright as a button. "So what's wrong with me again?", as if he were asking what time the party was. I take him through it.

"You remember the blood test? You passed that. Well done, you're through to the next round. The echocardiogram? Bing! You passed that too. Round three: the electrocardiogram. Full marks – on to the next level, Super Mario. Remember the cardiac catheterisation? Yet another pass – nothing can stop this kid now. And finally the heart biopsy – he's done it!

"What this means, my friend, is that you have something very rare called restrictive cardiomyopathy. That means that your heart – a muscle – isn't working properly, and it's not filling with blood in the way that it should because the walls inside the heart are too stiff.

"Things in your body that are meant to work for you actually sometimes work against you."

"So I'm basically fighting myself," he says.

"That's right. Now I know what you're asking – what's my prize? Well, the prize is – wait for it – a brand new heart. That's right; we're going to send you to sleep, open you up, pop it in, wake you up, and off you go! How does that sound?"

"Where's it going to come from?" he asks.

"Well, we'll take it from someone who doesn't need it any more."

"What if it's not the right size?"

"It will be, because we'll take it from someone just like you."

"Why don't *they* need it?"

"Because...they'll be dead, I'm afraid. Unlucky for them. Lucky for you."

But the boy doesn't get it. "Why would a *child* be *dead*?"

Scene Nine

ANNA I spend quite a bit of time imagining an alternative me, one that set off from the same point at the same time but made different decisions. A me that went to Oxford instead of Cambridge, that has all the same strengths but none of the weaknesses, that appears effortless and makes no mistakes.

The main attribute of this other me – the me that could have been – is that she's married to a colleague of Simon's called Matthew. That's the key difference. And she and Matthew have the most astonishing sex life, making love wildly every day or at least as often as I can come up here to the attic when Simon's not back from work yet, listening out for his key in the lock. I generally try to wear wool on these occasions, just a woollen jumper or something, which is cosy and makes me feel cuddly but which also has a certain scratch to it.

The literal part of me insists that I have to imagine everything through from the beginning, how we met, how Matthew arrived first instead of Simon, and so my eyes locked with *his* instead, and it all spins out from there. Actually, sometimes Simon doesn't arrive at all, we never meet, and in fact sometimes it's his parents who never meet, and he was never born, or they do and he was, but he was killed in the war. Desert Storm that would have to be, I suppose.

But anyway now it's just Matthew and I, and we live on the Cote d'Azur, from where he commutes in to Monaco every now and then. And there's a delicious irony, in that because of Matthew's international reputation and vast wealth no one would ever guess that once in the bedroom he effectively becomes my slave – he's there to serve me and me alone, and he instinctively knows that, and each time he not only fulfils my whim more completely but anticipates it more swiftly.

My goodness he's a magnificent lover, never tiring nor growing old, and on this occasion Sir Matthew hasn't even had time to undress, so urgent is my desire, he's still in white-tie and tails, with his Order of Merit and Nobel Prize medals banging against his chest. The helicopter can wait, he says. Anna; it's all about you, it's all about you. But just as I'm beginning to climax –

SIMON "What on earth are you *doing* up here?"

ANNA *(quickly)* "Pushing my hands into these old letters as a child does with autumn leaves."

And instantly, just as I'm almost there, Matthew melts away and is replaced by Simon. I have to be thinking of Simon when I come, that's just something I always have to do, it seems. It has to be Simon with his safe, well-meaning, husbandy smell of soap and faint shit. And I think back to the other me, the imaginary one, the relaxed, successful one. Surely *she* would be able to fantasise competently.

But while it lasts, it's wonderful. And ninety percent of nothing is, after all, better than nothing.

Scene Ten

JENNIFER By now the firm is holding enough of my own money for me to start wanting a bit of investment advice myself.

You're probably wondering why I don't have *Alex* as a boyfriend. He's a financial genius, of course, but he's also a total geek. The thin, academic type. It would be like making love to celery.

For Alex the stock exchange seems to be a route to revenge for something dreadful that must have happened years ago. I can only imagine it was sex-related, because he's one of those people who uses very aggressive sexual swear-words to describe the buying and selling of equities. He loves beating the big traders, the old, established firms, the stock market itself, Alex just loves to beat them all – or fuck them all, as he would obviously say.

He said to me: "Do you have a lover at the moment?"

And I said: Well, he's not a lover. He's a doctor.

And I think of all the men who have fantasised about me. They're all lonely too.

Alex isn't lonely, though. He's got money.

But then again, so have I.

Scene Eleven

SIMON We were in her stuffy, overheated flat. She was sitting on the prow of her bed, and when she started massaging her shoulder I realised she was only wearing four items of clothing. When the strap of one of her dangling shoes fell from her heel to the rug she was down to only three.

And then she stands up, doesn't say a word – this is out of nowhere – she just stands up and lifts her dress off over her head. Simple as that. As though she were alone, undressing while she watched TV.

But it's blinding, it's like a flash of light, and I almost put my hand up to shield my eyes. And I thought, no matter what I do now, no matter how long I live, I will always see that.

She forces my arms over my head, holding both my wrists.

And I dissolve into her like an aspirin into a swimming pool, fizzing and dispersing until there's nothing left, I'm gone, and every bit of pain I've ever had is smoothed away and everything is gone, perfectly gone and all the lights go out one by one until there's nothing left, there's nothing.

Even as I was doing it, it was as if it wasn't me doing it, I was just watching it, I was watching a film with someone else doing it. That's what killers say, apparently, explaining how it feels to pull the trigger.

And then, about halfway through, my phone starts buzzing, up on the table like a fly against the glass.

And she says, "Do you have to get that?"

And I say, "No."

And it just keeps on buzzing. But it does keep on buzzing.

Scene Twelve

ANNA I stand on the quay, and watch HMS Vengeance, one of our Vanguard-class nuclear submarines, push out of dock. An ink-black whale heading west, into the gloomy, faded sun, and heading down, down into the impenetrable slate of Loch Gare and out into the Atlantic.

I'm at Her Majesty's Naval Base Clyde, dressed a little inappropriately, I'm starting to think, since I've been asked for my ID about a dozen times now. This must be what people wear who are only pretending to be people like me.

This contributes to my sense of feeling a fraud, as though I'm smuggling in my intention to destroy the base, to turn this place into a ghost town by telling its dirty little secret to Parliament. I begin to wonder if there's a machine that can detect my moral quandary, and something somewhere is beeping.

Obviously the whole point of my being here is to steer me towards loyalty, loyalty to the project, to the mission.

The vessel takes to the flux, the brutal spray flinging about her, choppy and awful, and I long for her to sink fathom after fathom to safety in the alien totality of the water.

Sir Adam has kept the pressure up. At first he tried the professional approach: do I believe in Trident, do I want Britain to remain a nuclear player. Well, of course I do, yes. But...

Then he tries the personal approach. "It's a tightly-knit profession, you know. Testifying against us might be seen as a betrayal. I'd hate to see you struggling to find work," et cetera.

"But I wouldn't be testifying against anyone," I say. "I'd just be telling the truth."

I look at the riot of the ocean's surface. All that remains of the submarine is the tell-tale communication cable. I turn against the driving wind and head back.

On the way home I think about those poor submariners, so far from home, how they're prepared to kill for me, prepared to kill millions, and I feel a little surge of patriotism, a sort of confused, general nostalgia. I try to find a link between their mission and mine, between what they're asked to sacrifice and what I'm asked to sacrifice.

It wouldn't really be *lying*. Technically. It would just be delaying.

Feeling lost, I ring Simon, but I can't get hold of him. I let the phone ring and ring, it's quite late now, and when it goes to voicemail I hang up and ring again, and again it goes to voicemail and again I leave no message.

Scene Thirteen

JENNIFER His wife is away, and he takes me to Bath, to a hotel in a Georgian terrace. The kind of place where two pages of room service are devoted to food for your pet.

We don't leave the room for three days.

It's not how his body looks, it's how it makes me feel. When I'm in his arms I'm really small and safe. Like I'm underage.

We're both like adolescents, actually. Like the amount of time we spend kissing, that sort of desperate, end-in-itself kissing and afterwards my mouth feels how it used to after clarinet lessons; my lips numb from being pressed against my teeth so hard.

It's not enough for me to fuck him, to be fucked by him; I want to eat him, I literally want to push my teeth into him and chew, to swallow and absorb him.

I have brought with me to Bath the extended anthology of lingerie – a complete repertoire of profanity in cotton and lace; the 18-certificate box-set of haberdashery with director's cut and deleted scenes; the cappuccino and confetti and gingham and scarlet, the wires and straps and clips and cups, the plunges and ruches and balconettes, side-tie cache-sexe with cotton double-string. And bras with bows, the latter often favoured because they reinforce the suggestion that the breasts are a gift.

But he couldn't care less. He has about as much use for my underwear as a bear does for a can-opener. He just wants me naked. And that's exactly what I am.

He looks at me as if he's going to paint me, and I feel unzipped and gentle and exposed.

And afterwards, feral and spermy, I lie there, complete.

Later, he looks through my stuff, and thumbs through the thing I use for the business cards I receive – it's a cross between a Filofax and a photo album – and he stops at one, with four letters, M. R. L. K. embossed in very dark blue, and says "How on earth do you know him?"

On the drive back to London I make him stop after a few miles so I can buy five jars of local honeycomb from a farmer's stall by the side of the road.

"Who are *they* all for?" he asks.

"No one," I say. "I've got a Winnie-the-Pooh complex."

Scene Fourteen

SIMON A few weeks later the boy's parents are ushered in, like the Catholic bereaved to see the bishop. I've given the warning: I only have five minutes.

These two trust me so much they don't even want to know the details, they don't even ask, what's the probability, tell it to us straight, what's the deal with the boy, we can take it – or, as so many parents are these days, that knowing glare, the silent threat; get it right, friend, get this one right, or I'll sue the fuck out of you. Almost wanting me to fail so they can crush me.

But not these two. Oh no. They're hanging on. They've come this far via every point of optimism – perhaps it's only stress, perhaps it's only muscular, perhaps it's only skeletal, perhaps it's only a mild abnormality, perhaps it's only...but there aren't any "only"s after that; everything's potentially fatal now, everything's massive.

"Oh," they say, "we trust you, sir, we trust you," they say. I don't tell them about the superstitions, I don't tell them how it all comes down to how guilty I am, how lucky I feel. I just smile. And they smile, in that way that couples sometimes have with each other; how funny – oh, they'll laugh about this when they get home – the idea that I – *I* – could fail to save the life of their child.

Thank you for seeing us, says the father. Thank you.

And then, as they're leaving, he turns to his wife and says,

"There's nothing that man doesn't know about the heart."

Scene Fifteen

ANNA We're in the Saab and the brakes don't work and the drop of the cliff is just a few yards away. I'm free of the seatbelt and my hand's on the door and I'm still in with a chance if I jump now and roll but I look across at Simon and he can't undo his seatbelt, he's stuck. And I have two seconds to decide. Do I jump, so at least one of us survives, life is precious, it's what he would have wanted? Or is the moment of his death so critical that I have to be there for him, that's the one thing I *have* to do, it's the only true love there is, everything else is just habit and convenience and barter, and the six seconds we're about to share outweigh everything else that's ever happened to us.

I haven't yet made my decision, although I think about it every few days. I'm thinking of it now, in fact, as I go through the post while he sits across from me reading the Saturday *Telegraph*. Toast, marmalade, that lovely fluffy, almost chewy orange juice.

I'm actually prattling on about something else when I interrupt myself: Hello? What's this? It's a notice from the DVLA I've just opened, what's going on here? Apparently we owe a fine and points on the licence of the driver as we were photographed travelling at 86 miles per hour on the westbound section of the M4 just before the Junction 18 turn-off to Bath, and all this, I calculate out loud, the week I was in Frankfurt. What's going on?

Simon puts the newspaper down, totally serious.

And he looks at me, with this strange expression on his face that I don't think I've ever seen before, and he says, "OK. Just listen to what I've got to say, all right? Don't interrupt."

And I say, "OK..."

SIMON "Matthew has left his wife. He just...they...they just were trying to work it out, and then they stopped trying to work it out and then... He just wanted to get away for a couple of days, he was totally lost and didn't know what was going

on, and I said he could take the car and get out of London
to clear his head and have a bit of a think. Obviously he
drove like a madman down to Bath or whatever, but...there
you go. I didn't want to... I don't know... I just didn't think
to say anything."

Quick as a flash. Afterwards I tried to understand how it
was that I was able to think of this so quickly. It was as if
I'd been preparing the story for weeks, perhaps even as I
was at the wheel of the car.

In broad terms it was true – Matt *had* left his wife recently,
he was a serial adulterer in that brazen way that makes you
think his wife somehow knew, although as it turned out she
didn't. And the timing did just about match up.

But when I saw Anna was going to go for it, that she believed
the whole thing, it was like watching a flame spread across
a sheet of paper. And all she said was:

ANNA Did he leave her or did she leave him?

SIMON What difference does it make? And then she gets
totally sidetracked, as if she's completely forgotten about
the fine, about the ticket and the whole event, and she
starts...*worrying* about Matthew; is he doing all right, is
he upset, where's he living now... And of course the relief is
coming off me in waves, although it's not exactly relief, it's
more a sense of my own power, that I know how to control
things. Buoyed by this, I suggest that we get Matt round
for dinner so we can mop him up and check he's OK and
give him some decent food.

ANNA Do I spend time thinking about the tragedy of a failed
marriage, of what's to become of the wife – who, all too late,
I realise I haven't been asking any questions about? No. All
I feel is a giddy tremor at the sudden possibility of it all.

I must also confess to a previous incident with Matthew
at the three-quarters point of a drinks evening at Simon's
work four years ago, when the room was pretty crowded
but probably not crowded enough to warrant the exuberant

moment of frottage-by-proxy I received as he tried to move behind me to get to the warmed crab cakes. I pushed my bottom into him ever so discreetly and felt his chest against me, and I thought his face lingered around my hair to breathe it in.

Later that evening Matthew made a very ambiguous remark as we were leaving, which at the time I didn't construe as a come-on but in my daily retrospects has become nothing but that.

Scene Sixteen

SIMON After breakfast I went out on the Heath on my own. There was no one around and I just dumbly wandered about, God knows what I was doing. There was this weird sense of reluctance in the air, I didn't want to be anywhere and I was exhausted, and I thought, you know, I'm not really enjoying any of this. Actually. Not *really*.

I have a mistress. I'm one of those men who has a mistress. It doesn't sound like me. I try to picture her, I think of us together, like scissors; meeting and cutting and pulling away, meeting and cutting and pulling away.

My new thing is music. This time last year I could take it or leave it. Now it's an absolute fucking prerequisite. I'd say I spend about two hundred quid a week on CDs and on iTunes. Stuff I'd never heard of before. And it's amazing. Bach's *St John Passion*, Liszt's *Soirée de Vienne*. George Frederick Handel's *Eternal Source of Light Divine*.

(We hear the last of these.)

Scene Seventeen

JENNIFER Someone from the *Wall Street Journal* wants to write a book about Alex, and though Alex pretends not to be excited I can tell he is. Next month they're going to watch him in action, they're paying for us to fly over, to see Alex at the New York Stock Exchange, a photo opportunity for the cover and promoting the book; "This is where it all started...", how he does it, the master at work, the alchemist.

He keeps referring back to the book, even here while we wait in the lobby for a meeting with the senior partners of a firm so rich and influential you won't have heard of it. He starts to mention the book again, then stops himself with a panicky little blush.

"Get over it, Alex," I say. "It's only a book. Do you know how many of those there are out there?"

I'm really here to add glamour. I certainly can't talk about bonds. They won't let me. And yes, I'm a little bit in awe of the surroundings, which even for the type of place this is are pretty opulent.

Alex has nothing but contempt for these people, though. We're going to fuck them, he inevitably says. Yes, Alex, I say, yes; we're going to fuck them, that's right. Then I say: Do you not have any loyalty to anyone, Alex? I mean, these are good people who want to work with us.

Alex snorts. Loyalty, he says, went out with Times New Roman. It's about control.

And I look up at all the oil paintings of former chairmen, now all deceased and I think: you're all dead now, and I'm alive, I'm in the middle of it, I'm free. There's this beam of light gradually moving across the history of the world, just a tight, narrow shaft of light and it's illuminating me – and all my fellow specks of dust – and we're alive, until the light moves on and we return to an infinity of blackness. But now, right now, I'm in the light. And I'm making the most of it.

Scene Eighteen

SIMON There was a guy I used to work with who couldn't go ten seconds without clearing his throat. He was like a smoke alarm with a low battery warning, it was unbearable. It would've actually been better if he only hawked every five seconds, because then you wouldn't've had the chance to forget about it. But as it was you heard it, you were repulsed by it for about three seconds, then you slowly forgot about it over the next four seconds, you'd have about three seconds of tranquillity, and then suddenly – oh, God, yeah, I remember, here it is again.

That's how it is with me now, except I don't clear my throat, I think about having sex with Jennifer. The weather of my mind is just a non-stop fucking drizzle – literally: a drizzle of fucking, an incessant rain of pornography, the images of her streaming down the back of my mind in the way that the phlegm would stream down the back of that guy's trachea.

I've stored up these images with the male penchant for hoarding, an enthusiasm previously limited in my case to Second World War memorabilia, trophies which ironically have proved to be far less malignant.

I'm having sex with her right now, in fact. I'm inside her and trying not to come, and it's these moments that are my only bearable moments – not because at last I'm experiencing what I'm always thinking about, but because it's only when I'm experiencing it I don't have to think about it.

There are no more surprises now, no little delights left to discover. Sex offers all the thrill of a nicotine patch. I use it to clamber back up to zero for a few brief moments of total stillness before the horror starts all over again.

I'm almost there, and I begin to think how hopeless this whole thing is, how unwinnable, our sexual history; just one long retreat from joy. Being with her isn't enough, dominating her isn't enough, making her love me isn't enough. I could spend every waking moment fucking her, I could be four men fucking her simultaneously for the rest of my life and I couldn't remove one atom of this thing. There's me, there's her, and there's my desire for her. And the three have nothing to do with each other.

I also can't help noticing I drink quite a bit these days for someone who doesn't drink.

I feel myself hate her, and it's the most vivid sensation – beautiful, really. I look up and see next to the bed a lamp on a marble stand, and I imagine using it to cave in her skull, lifting up the green-felted base and slamming it down into her dumb, astonished face, forcing it into her again and again. And for a moment I can feel something; I'm no longer numb. And it's unbelievable.

And as this thought courses through me I at last join the rollercoaster.

Afterwards, still in our grim hotel – an airport hotel without an airport – we're waiting for the rain to stop so we can make a dash for the tube. I go to sign the bill, and I realise the nib of my Mont Blanc has been bent back, way back, it's up like this, as though someone's pressed down on it as hard as they could.

I say: "Have you seen this?"

JENNIFER "What?"

SIMON Totally innocent.

She used it last. I know she did, I happened to look over the other day and see her using it – hadn't asked to borrow it or anything – she was just messing around with it, like a kid. It's almost as if it's been done deliberately, spitefully.

I say: "Don't lie to me. Did you fuck up my pen?"

I look at her, as she pretends to read her moronic paperback. There's an obviousness in her shape, I see now, a sort of physical sleaziness. I'd be embarrassed if anyone saw us together – even strangers, I mean.

And there she sits, not saying a word, not giving a damn, with her pretty little eyes tracing over the page.

JENNIFER He's suddenly there, in front of me, with a blackness about him, a deadness, he's almost shaking. And he just stands there, staring at me as though he's about to spit. And he says:

SIMON "This was a present from Anna. You know that, don't you?" And she says:

JENNIFER "No, I didn't know that, actually." He says:

SIMON "Are you proud of yourself?"

JENNIFER And I say: Of course not.

And that's the first time I hear him say her name.

Scene Nineteen

ANNA I'm awake, and I have this odd foreboding.

Yesterday, Sir Adam asked me "Do you really think the integrity of one person is worth thirty thousand jobs?"

I spend ten minutes building up to turning on the light. When I do so I imagine the flash of light is the first wave from the bomb, and for a split-second we're at the centre of the centre, it's just one phosphorescent imprint before oblivion, we're two of ten million blown out like candles, no time even to scream and no traces of us left, wiped out of the collective memory as the nervy pulse of a continent is replaced with an emptiness, an absence decaying backwards from nothing.

I have the overwhelming urge to wake Simon, to tell him, to say, child-like, "I don't know what to do."

And he would think it through out loud, as he does, using calming, logical phrases such as "first principles". And then he'd say "What do *you* think?", and I'd feel important and intelligent and loved.

I turn off the light, and watch the shape of Simon's back as it rises and falls against the gloom.

Scene Twenty

JENNIFER Simon finished with me. He finished me. He told me he didn't want to see me again. Just like that.

I asked him why. He said:

SIMON "I don't know."

JENNIFER I said, why are you doing this? He said:

SIMON "I don't know."

JENNIFER I said, if you don't know *why* you're doing it, why are you *doing* it? And he said:

SIMON "I don't know."

JENNIFER I've put on weight, I've lost weight.

When I watch the TV, I don't actually watch it, I just sit there looking at the three blinking zeroes on the DVD player below.

When eating, I can't let the cutlery touch my mouth. I carefully scrape the food off the fork with my teeth, keeping a thin film of food between me and the metal.

I do sleep every now and then, but it's more like a series of little snatches of forgetfulness, after which my mouth tastes like the colour grey.

To relax, I Google his name, and the first screen of results is as familiar to me as the opening page of choral evensong in my old prayer book. Like a lot of men his age he doesn't have a massive internet presence, and the first reference that's really about him is five down, but I've also grown fond of the most prominent others who share his name: the bullish real estate salesman in Florida with his macrobiotic wife, the grinning Exeter University undergraduate and his increasingly controversial chairmanship of the guitar club – they're like family to me now. But the few precious pages that are of him – the hospital website, the professional association biography, the blurred back-row presence in the rugby team photo circa 1998; these are the relics and the icons of my religion, and when the pleasure of these dims, even just the shape of letters that make up his name gives me a brief quickening before my mind swims on, groggy, jetlagged, furring like a kettle.

On the tube, I'll sometimes look at an attractive man, and he'll look back at me. We look at each other until he gets off at his stop, and when he goes I think, we could have had a child together, and that child will never exist now. And parts of me fly off in every direction, like sparks. And when he's on the platform I always think: if he looks back at me the child would've been a boy.

I remember from school: when the Romans finally conquered Carthage, it wasn't retribution enough for them to destroy every building stone by single stone. The soldiers then ploughed over the city and sowed salt into the earth so nothing could ever live or grow there again.

I gravitate to his house, to the house of Simon, my former lover, the man who loved me once. I push myself against the railings of the private garden in the Crescent, I watch the lights of his house go on as night falls and the tableau moves silently from one room to another.

I asked him why. He said:

SIMON "I don't know."

JENNIFER I said, why are you doing this? He said:

SIMON "I don't know."

JENNIFER I said, if you don't know *why* you're doing it, why are you *doing* it? And he said:

SIMON "I don't know."

Scene Twenty-One

ANNA I'm ready. I'm sitting there, in front of the Select Committee. There's eight of them. And one of me.

After some preliminaries, easily batted back, they get to the key question, the big question, the question that will make me who I am.

In your expert, professional opinion – they say – how likely is it that the initial figures here (waving our document) will prove to represent the real cost of the missile system?

I pause for a moment and, in my mind's eye, I see myself journeying from here to King's Cross, to the offices of the *Guardian*. I announce myself at the desk and a journalist comes down and gives me a hug and some awful coffee in a polystyrene cup and tells me that I'm taking the most incredible stand, I'm the whistleblower of the year, and even better, he says, not to be cynical about it, but you're an attractive woman, and I say, oh, I'm not, I'm not...

And, yes, I lose my job, I never work in the nuclear industry again, but I have my principles. I'm intact. I teach, I turn around an inner-city school and a new generation of young people learn not just Chemistry A-Level but the meaning of bravery, and honesty, and integrity.

But that's not what I do. I lie. I confirm the old figures, I cover up our mistakes, I obscure our trail. I keep quiet. I pretend everything's OK.

And it doesn't even feel like a lie. It feels lucid and flawless, unquestionably the right thing to do.

Afterwards I spend some time back in the office, shredding, and I have some ultra-sensitive stuff in my case with me now, which I'm going to burn in the front room grate when I get in.

But Sir Adam, of course, shines when he looks at me. He tells his driver to take me home, and here, in the back of the car, I relax into the seat like an ambassador and watch London scud by as flecks of snow spin about us.

And I think: I'm totally alone, I'm the only one who knows. I look at the advent crowds, and imagine them thanking me, and I say, "You're welcome. You're welcome," as though I'm dispensing coins.

As we stop at traffic lights I watch a young couple holding each other in an elegant, passionate embrace. They look perfect; perfectly good-looking, perfectly happy, perfect for each other, like that famous black-and-white French photo of a kissing couple I had on my study wall in Sixth Form. I imagine this couple getting engaged tonight, and married in the summer, and how they'll take their blond children in little blazers to church every Sunday morning.

"Look at them!" I say with delight, and it's only as the driver turns that I notice – too late – a detail in the canvas; the woman's hand is inside the man's trousers at the front, methodically plunging up and down with the piston of her fist.

The driver studies them for a moment. "Yes," he says. "It's alright for some."

Scene Twenty-Two

JENNIFER The New York Stock Exchange. Five degrees below freezing.

The flight over actually helped. Wrapped in the warm fleece of Tramadol, I looked out over the Atlantic and every seven seconds ticked off another mile from London. I loosen even as Alex, across from me, endlessly distractable, tightens up.

We meet with the *Wall Street Journal* writer and photographer and now we're here, we're suddenly here, and this is our chance to see Alex in action, the wonder boy, turning yet more money into yet more money.

The bell sounds, and trading may now commence. Our new friends are excited, and I realise I am too. I look over at Alex, and look away, then quickly look back. He's leaning forward rather drastically; no, more than that – it's sort of like he's falling slowly, and then he pulls himself up again, the way you do if you're falling asleep on a train. He starts twitching and shaking and so of course I assume he's on drugs. I say, "What's the matter?"

And he looks at me, white as a sheet, and says, "I've never done this before."

I say, "Never done what before?"

"Traded."

"What are you talking about, Alex?"

And he just says, "I'm sorry."

He can't look at me, he can't look at anyone, he just starts walking off, and then he turns around and says, "I'm sorry... I'm sorry."

And everything I've been trying to get away from is pushed back into me, as though I'm being forced to swallow a glass of sand.

I call out after him – "So where the fuck is everybody's money?"

He says one word, and it's the last word I ever hear him say.
"Gone."

Scene Twenty-Three

SIMON I get the call, and I run to the car. They have the heart, it's ready for me, packed in ice.

By the time I arrive the anaesthetist has completed. The boy's under, he's scrubbed and unconscious, waiting.

There is just one complication which I should mention. I have been drinking.

Up until about an hour before the operation I still thought I could get through it OK. I'm not that bad. And there's still quite a while to go yet.

It's not brain surgery.

It was only twenty minutes before prep that I realised I was stuck. Stupidly I actually started drinking again at that point. I think my logic was...well, there was no logic, but I did really need a drink. I had a bottle of Glenlivet in my office which Pete Brunson had given me, and I tucked into that to the tune of about a quarter of a pint, just to catch my breath and help me think.

And that drink does help, oddly, it really helps. I'm steady now, but I can feel the Scotch scurrying through me, spreading out in me like an unclenching fist, and I'm unfolding, my brain sort of bursts open like a firework.

So by the time I'm in the theatre I've drunk around three quarters of a pint of Scotch.

I mean, when you say it like that it sounds...but at the time...there just wasn't enough time. I could have asked John Walters to do it instead, but I'm hardly going to say "John, I'm drunk, do the op for me." I just couldn't think of any plausible excuse. I could have said I was ill, I suppose. Believe it or not that just didn't occur to me.

I take the scalpel, and I push it into the boy.

Slowly I slice open his chest. I pull back the curtains of flesh to the splashy, velvet bedlam.

Now we're all leaning over, I'm in the centre of it. I've separated the pericardium membrane and started to dissect the great vessels to get him onto cardiopulmonary bypass.

I'm trying to think clearly, but it's as though every thought is covered in wet fur. At one point my mouth unaccountably fills with saliva and I'm convinced I'm going to have to spit it over the boy, and my stomach lurches as though it's falling out of my body, as though it were me who was cut open, but at the same time my feet are racing towards me, like I'm standing in a lift shooting upwards.

And I just think, OK, get a grip. No one suspects a thing. Just be relaxed. Then I start to think: am I over-relaxed? I might be. I might be. Tighten up a bit. The main thing is normal. Got to be normal.

The boy is lying there, except it's not the boy, it's just his body. It's only his body, and all I have to do now is transect a portion of his left atrium.

For a moment it's in my hand, my fingers have curled underneath it and I'm holding a heart, a resilient, defiant life.

I move on.

By now I begin to feel like I'm doing the whole thing on a boat, there's a subtle fuzz to everything.

I look up and immediately a nurse looks away, as if she's noticed. When she looks back at me I find myself winking at her – where on earth did that idea come from?

And then – I wasn't the first to see it, I hear someone in the room give a little gasp, and there's a general start back, a whiff of panic, just a small shift but enough to make me scan for whatever the fuck's happened, and then I see it, an angry streak of blood shooting out over his lower ribs.

And at that very second it becomes clear. If I tell Anna about the affair, if I come clean, then the boy will live. And if I don't, he'll die.

Scene Twenty-Four

ANNA Simon's due back in about half an hour, and he says Matthew's going to be here at eight.

So. I'm doing a chicken with lemon-and-rosemary roast potatoes, and I've made a gravy from the stock. I do always feel that a roasting chicken makes a house smell wonderfully safe. There's roasted root vegetables and garlics and a white sauce for the cauliflower. Also an Australian wine, one bottle in the fridge and one on the table. I made a chocolate sponge last night, and this is on the stove in its steamer, custard all ready to prepare on the worktop.

There's a piece of music by Ella Fitzgerald I want playing when Matthew gets here; I've got it cued up on the CD player but obviously I can't press play until the doorbell goes, so for now I listen to *Just A Minute* on Radio 4 – a repeat, I think. You've got to hand it to those guys; they're so clever, they really are. And after that I switch over to Radio 3 for the semi-finals of *Young Musician of the Year*. Just lovely.

And then Simon gets in, I hear the door and his muffled announcement and up he goes to shower and change, I presume, and so for the very last few moments I'm all alone, and I slowly walk around the kitchen, and put my hands on the back of the chair where Matthew will sit and I imagine he's already sitting there, and I'm rubbing his shoulders and lovingly checking his scalp for signs of dandruff or balding.

JENNIFER This is the street. Somewhere a piano is being practised, and a few houses already have their Christmas trees up. But here we are, this is the door, solid as 10 Downing Street. I need to count down, to silently count backwards for the impetus to push the bell, and as I do so it's like I'm falling towards it, the door is streaming towards me and I put my finger on the bell almost to keep me upright as the adrenaline tears through me.

ANNA I start up and almost race to it, and have to stop and remind myself. Just at that moment Simon's coming downstairs, and we both get to the door at the same time, and I open it.

JENNIFER And Matt says, Hi. This is Jennifer.

SIMON And she goes to shake my hand.

ANNA Why's he with a girl? He didn't say he was bringing a girl. Why's he with a girl? And my heart drops like a stone. And then I feel a huge wave of sympathy for Matthew. He's obviously lonely, why shouldn't he be with someone young and pretty? Of course he would be with a girl, why would he not be? What girl wouldn't want to be with him? And I realise I'm just one of a million, I'm nothing, he's never even noticed me. I'm a zero at the back of the queue, a queue of who knows how many women all dreaming of Matthew and his private practice and the small scar that runs across his left cheek.

SIMON She's looking at me, defiantly, she doesn't take her eyes off me; eyes that go all the way back to God. And I look at Matt, practically rubbing his plump, successful and no doubt still-cunty fingers together, rejoicing at his dumb luck; I look at him and I realise he doesn't have a clue – perhaps for the very first time in his life – he really doesn't have a clue.

Even on the bridge when Oscar died he gave off this officious, non-surpriseable aura of knowing exactly what the fuck he was doing, as though he was unfazed, as though it was all part of the plan, as if Oscar was desperate to do it and we tried to stop him, which incidentally was the story Matt told police in a turn of events he's never referred to since. I look at him, so proud of his conquest he's not talking so much as gurgling. Funny.

He doesn't know what's going on.

And then I think – actually, nor do I.

JENNIFER The dinner really was just chance. Once I remembered that Simon knew Matthew and I still had Matthew's card from the lunchtime date at the restaurant, I just wanted Simon to find out about me, to hear I was seeing his friend, and I wanted this to hurt him, the knowledge that now Matthew was my lover, my unwitting lover, my brutal revenge-fuck. But then came the invitation to dinner, the call to prayer, and Matthew was my Trojan horse, my American Airlines Flight 11, and I had the means, I had the route, a red carpet straight between the two pillars and into the hall.

SIMON Neither Matt nor Anna suspects a thing, of course, and in a strange way this unites them, although they don't know it. I briefly imagine them together, as if *they* were the couple.

JENNIFER If there's Sally at one end and Miriam at the other, she's about an Emma. You know; she seemed one of those people who's read the books they're meant to have read, and likes the films she's meant to like. This is the woman he chose, in the house he chose. I'd have chosen a different house. If it was me.

ANNA Is this girl why he left his wife? I start to think less of her until I realise it's not disapproval so much as envy.

JENNIFER I'll give the woman this, though; she gave the smallest hint that she instinctively knew what I represented – just a single raised eyebrow as she was turning away, which if it were in speech form would have come out as an "oh, really". I didn't think she had it in her. As we're ushered through and she makes the drinks I take my revenge by convincing her there's no such thing as a lime, it's just an unripened lemon.

SIMON I close the heavy door and look around me. By the time I return the other two are in the drawing room; it's just Anna here in the kitchen on her own.

ANNA Back in the kitchen the chicken looks back at me with nothing but sarcasm. Simon's actually quite sweet about it – of course he's got no idea why I'm really upset – but he's so sweet and concerned, and he says, yes, that is a little rude of Matt, isn't it, to bring someone else unannounced, and I say yes, well he always was a little fucking rude, wasn't he – it just came out of me, God knows why, and I start crying. I turn away, but I start crying. And he puts his hands round my waist, which makes me feel terribly guilty and I cry all the more in a useless, snotty way trying to think how this will look if they come in now, and Simon just keeps saying "What's the matter? What's the matter?" and I feel his breath on my neck and his fingers knotted together at my stomach.

I realise how stupid I am; why on earth would I be happier if someone else had their arms round me instead of him? How would that help? I know I should tell him everything, but I don't, I just say "There's not going to be enough chicken now," and, heartbreakingly, he says "Don't give me any. I'll just have potatoes." And he kisses me. And I say:

I love you.

And he says: / I love you too.

SIMON / I love you too. And then I feel Matt enter the room behind me, and he starts filling the room with yet more congratulations on how the boy's operation turned out, that I'm a genius, that no other doctor could have done what I'd done, or at least no more than one in a hundred, he's careful to moderate it down to that, the begrudging little prick. And I leave him, I walk off because I can't hear all that any more, I'm sick of it, I'm sick of my success.

ANNA Matthew stays, it's just him and me now, this is the moment I've been waiting for. He's talking to me, explaining how he met Jennifer – is it Jennifer? – and I am listening, I'm trying to listen, but actually I'm beginning to find Matthew a little annoying, there's something facile and crass about him that I've never noticed before – he can see I'm upset, but he chooses to ignore it, and he goes on instead about how it's all a terrible shame, it's a dreadful shame, this poor girl, this poor Jennifer – yes, it is Jennifer – all the problems of the firm, a total shock, caught up in a Ponzi scheme, the ring-leader still on the run in the US, and she's ruined, of course, the girl's ruined.

And I want to say *she's* ruined? How about all those hardworking, honest people who lost everything? But I keep quiet.

No one believes she wasn't involved, he says, and oh, the indignity of being arrested et cetera. I mean do I think she's a thief? Do I? And he stops. I say:

I don't know. I was always told you could tell a thief by the way they look at you.

That's good enough for him, apparently, and on he goes.

SIMON This can't be some grisly coincidence. It's some sort of forlorn attempt to get back at me, to show me that she doesn't need me, to prove she's moved on. She's there, standing there in the drawing room, she couldn't look more out of place if she was a goat. I say, what are you doing?

JENNIFER I said, "I'm not doing anything. I'm really not doing anything." And he said, Good, because I don't want you fucking things up.

SIMON And, unbelievably, with all the flourish of a heroin addict, she tries to undo my fly.

JENNIFER He said please, just...just please. And he pushes me away and leaves the room. I'm alone, left to wander up the stairs, lined as they are with shelves full of nineteenth-century adultery novels, and I pretend to study the titles as I climb.

SIMON In the time it takes to return to the kitchen I realise this is the moment I have to tell her, to tell Anna about the affair. It's all in this sort of rush now, I've got that focus you get in the two seconds before you vomit – and here it comes.

ANNA Matthew is still wittering on, and now I'm fabricating invisible tasks at the stove because my smile's become so painfully fixed. Jennifer – and now the name's really beginning to grate – Jennifer's bail was fixed at two million, and they were lucky to get that, because she was originally deemed a flight risk, but they raised it in three days, an excellent lawyer, apparently, and I'm on the brink of saying please, be quiet, just be quiet, and then here he is, suddenly, here is my husband, now standing there, quietly there, and I feel rescued, as if I were a child being picked up by him, lifted into the air, out of the way of all harm.

JENNIFER Up in their bedroom I prowl and snoop; the place is like a museum. As predicted, she's the kind of woman who has a couple of fluffy toy rabbits on the bedside to make up for the absence of offspring, but they strike a wrong note, somehow, and there's generally something a little too dusted about the place, as though it's not real, it's all staged. I start to go through the bedside drawers, hoping to learn for example what contraception they use. And that's when I find it, stashed there, as comforting and sympathetic and chunky as a kilo of chocolate.

SIMON I think: here goes. Here goes. And they stop and look at me, and I think, if I don't tell her now I'll never tell her – it's now or never, and all I have to do is say the words.

And I steady myself. And I start. I say:

There's something... Look. I have to tell you something.

JENNIFER One night when I was about twelve, I went to bed without putting any pyjamas on or a night-dress or anything – I've no idea why; just a whim. I wore absolutely nothing and it was the first time I'd ever been naked in bed, and I caught a glimpse of this life, this other life, this sense that my body could be a source of pleasure, and I felt like a film star and I stretched myself out, straightening my four little limbs to the furthest reaches of the sheets, where the linen was still cold, out into the vastness, the familiar vastness of the bed.

And back in the bedroom of my former lover and his wife, my former lover who now it seems won't even let me suck his cock I sit here holding his Nazi pistol, his antique, swastika'd firearm. I don't know anything about guns, frankly, although I have put it in my mouth – I know that much – and I squeeze the trigger – and I brace myself – but it's really resistant, it's not working, so I try it again, the rusty tang of the tip all the while in my tightening mouth, and I try it now with two fingers, squeezing the trigger more firmly and ah; here it comes, this is it, and it's the strangest f-

End

THIS
IS
NOT
THE
END

**Visit samuelfrench.co.uk
and discover the best
theatre bookshop
on the internet**

A vast range of plays
Acting and theatre books
Gifts

Lightning Source UK Ltd.
Milton Keynes UK
UKOW01f1651260717
306107UK00001B/34/P